To Start an Orchard

To Start an Orchard

poems

Michael Hettich

Press 53
Winston-Salem

Press 53, LLC
PO Box 30314
Winston-Salem, NC 27130

First Edition

Copyright © 2019 by Michael Hettich

All rights reserved, including the right of reproduction in whole or in part in any form except in the case of brief quotations embodied in critical articles or reviews. For permission, contact publisher at editor@Press53.com, or at the address above.

Cover Art, "Maw," 30 x 22-inch oil on panel
Copyright © 2015 by Jim Muehlemann
Used by permission of the artist

Author Photo by Colleen Hettich

Cover design by Kevin Morgan Watson and Christopher Forrest

Library of Congress Control Number
2019945899

Printed on acid-free paper
ISBN 978-1-950413-13-3

To the memory of John Hettich (1956–2015)

Many thanks to the editors of the following journals, where versions of these poems first appeared:

Alaska Quarterly Review, "The Shells"
Apalachee Review, "The Skin"
Architrave, "The Tree"
Cave Wall, "The 20th Century"
Commonweal, "The Ghost Trees"
The Comstock Review, "The Blizzard" & "The Lion"
The Florida Review, "The Light of Ancient Stars"
Great River Review, "The Horses," "The Milky Way" & "The Journey Home"
Green Linden, "The Apple Trees," "The Afternoon Nap" & "The Lucky One"
Hamilton Stone Review, "Soup" & "The Shirt"
Helen, "The Scarecrow" & "The Edge of the World"
Kestrel, "Starting from Sleep"
Mudfish, "First Love"
Mudlark, "Nature Poem," "The Hike" & "The Mica-Daughter"
New Madrid, "The Truth of Poetry"
Notre Dame Review, "The Secret Language," "To Blow Away like Mist" & "The Lesson"
Off the Coast, "Dream of Myself as an Only Child"
Pinyon, "The Dance"
Ploughshares, "The Windows"
Poetry East, "The Falls" & "Marimba"
Prairie Schooner, "To Start an Orchard"
Slant, "The Deer"
Sleet, "The Adjustment" & "Tango"
South Florida Poetry Journal, "The Retreat," "The Ghosts" & "The Pure Necessity"
Spillway, "The Thieves"
Split Rock Review, "The Pond"
Terrain.org, "Extinction," "Big Bend," "Constellation" & "Routine Weather"

"The Shells" was included in a collaborative, handmade book entitled *Conversation Too*, designed and printed by Tom Virgin

"The Mica-Daughter" was written in collaboration with artist Jenny Brillhart and included in the Sweat Broadside Project

"The Apple Tree" was printed as a broadside by Green Linden Press

"The Milky Way," "To Start an Orchard" & "To Blow Away like Mist" were reprinted by *Blue Heron Review* as the Blue Heron Speaks Featured Author for January, 2018

"The Shells" & "The Horses" were reprinted as a "Poetry Feature" by *PoetryMagazine.com*

"Nature Poem" was reprinted in *Visiting Bob: 100 Poems for Bob Dylan* (New Rivers Press, 2018)

"The Pure Necessity" was reprinted in *Voices from the Fierce Intangible World: Ten Years of the South Florida Poetry Journal*

"Extinction" & "The Milky Way," appeared in different forms in *The Frozen Harbor*, published by Red Dragonfly Press in 2017

"Soup" was reprinted in *KYSO*

"The Milky Way," "Before it Grows too Dark," "The Windows" & "To Blow Away, Like Mist" were reprinted in *Redux*

"Extinction," "Constellation," "To Blow Away, Like Mist," "The Ghost Trees," "Starting from Sleep," "The Horses," "Big Bend" & "The Hike" were reprinted in *Ginosko*

"Big Bend," "The Milky Way" & "The Light of Ancient Stars" were reprinted in *ArLiJo* (Gival Press)

"To Start an Orchard" was reprinted by *Poetry East*

Contents

I.

Big Bend	3
Extinction	4
Dream of Myself as an Only Child	5
Marimba	6
The Hike	7
The Milky Way	8
To Blow Away like Mist	9
The Ghost Trees	10
The Secret Language	11
The Horses	12
Scarecrow	13
The Blizzard	14
The Truth of Poetry	15
The Light of Ancient Stars	16

II.

Constellation	19
The Shells	20
To Start an Orchard	21
The Thieves	22
The Edge of the World	23
The Skin	24
The Afternoon Nap	25
Tango	26
The Lesson	27
The Retreat	28
First Love	29
Routine Weather	30
The Lion	31
The Windows	32
The Mica-Daughter	33
Nature Poem	34
The Pure Necessity	36

III.

The House	41
Soup	42
The Adjustment	43
The Pond	44
The Dance	45
The Stars	46
The Apple Trees	47
The Deer	48
The Lucky One	50
The Tree	52
The Falls	53
The Shirt	54
The 20th Century	55
The Journey Home	56

*

Starting From Sleep	59
Acknowledgments	61
About the Author	63
About the Cover Artist	65

A light in which there is no permanence, a light of nothing longer than a glimpse.
>   —John Berger, "Opening a Gate"

I.

Big Bend

Driving through the desert, we think of the children
deciding to lie down for a rest, holding hands.
We wonder at their parents. We are driving to the river,
cool and relaxed, squinting in the early sun
despite our dark glasses. We want to touch the river,
maybe wade there, lie down in the cool water
and let ourselves be carried down river. We want to
echo our voices against the canyon walls.
We think of the children, and their parents, setting out
across the wide desert, still cool and dripping
from crossing the river. Sheep graze on the other side
as we sit in the shade of the canyon, cool
from the river though the day's already burning
and somewhere the children are walking, holding hands,
thinking of the river, their parents, and home
as they look across the desert and seem to see a river
quivering the air like a dream. We are driving,
cool and refreshed and talking of our plans
for when we get home from the desert; we are listening
to music or news of what's happened far away
but we're thinking of the river and the canyon, and of
the children walking slowly, holding each other
across the wide desert, alone.

Extinction

The creature my mother had been once was hiding
in a supermarket magazine photograph, as though
she were a stylish shoe; the animal my father
had fancied as *himself*
was howling at the moon
like the wolf in that famous ad campaign
that taught us how to act both wild and stylish,
like a new kind of gesture. We had lost all the creatures
that weren't of our ilk, like we'd lost certain aunts
and uncles to their snapshots. And then we started losing
those animals inside us, as our sleep started dreaming
in languages of follicle and cuticle, fingernail
and ear wax, sand and snot—until something
moved around inside again, wilder than we'd ever been
and almost as vivid as the world, and it hurt
like language must have done once, or maybe even love.

Dream of Myself as an Only Child

I was heading outside to play in the rain
which had been falling for days, when my mother
called from her bath. She was reading and needed
a towel for her book. The bubbles, like blisters
around her body, were frothy and blue,
and their sweet scent made me think of an animal
caught in the body of a person who'd been sleeping
too long to be human anymore, someone
who might have turned over on his side while he slept
and simply disappeared. I closed the bathroom door
and went out to wander the sidewalk, collecting
worms that had drowned in the rain, searching
for dry spots on the front stoops to leave them for the birds,
as the trains flew by underground. I watched
the puddles shiver and imagined my father
down there, coming home; he was dozing, dreaming
of some other life and would sleep through his stop,
while my mother emerged from her bath to wander
the apartment in robe and perfume, waiting,
as I waited for the birds to notice the worms
I'd left them, and the puddles disappeared, into
the ground while the evening erased things, one by one.

Marimba

The man I wish I'd had the gumption to become
back when I was green and restless
requested that when he finally let go
his bones be fashioned into a kind of xylophone
and that the rest of him be buried
by the lake he loved.
He wished that his bones be played
on chilly autumn evenings when loons called
and leaves whispered a leathery language
as the wind prepared them to let go.
Beside the lake his sons could make a fire
and burn his clothes and books,
then roast whatever they could catch and feast.
But he died before I noticed, fell away
as a propped-up scarecrow falls from his scaffold
or the way memories fall from our minds
and become like small animals, mice or voles,
that know there are hungry owls in the woods
but can't stand to stay in their cramped nests any longer
and need to take a look at the moon.

The Hike

I decided to walk a big circle that day
to see what I could see. It felt good to have a body
after weeks at the desk; it felt good to saunter
alone, not talking except in my head,
maybe singing a little. If there were crows
cawing I'd reply, I thought, and if a deer
watched from the trees, maybe I would see it,
as I knew I'd see breezes moving through the grasses,
as I knew I'd see spiderwebs. Maybe I'd sit down
and read or write a little. If I could just open
myself a little wider, I thought, I might be something
instead of just someone, for a little while.
I might even try to stand still for an hour,
or lie down off the path where no one could see me
and pretend to dry up and blow away. I could be
a gesture signaling through the trees. Watch me
move as emptiness through the energetic air
like a glint you didn't see, but thought you did.

The Milky Way

If we could imagine that every word we speak
were an animal or insect, the last of a species
ever to be born, that the very act of speaking
brought extinction even before our words
had been heard and replied to, we might get a feeling
for the vanishings we witness but don't see. And if every
conversation were understood as a kind
of holocaust denuding whole landscapes, some people
would simply fall silent—as far as they could—
while most others would keep chattering on. Just imagine
the vast forests of lives, the near-infinity of forms
brought to a halt with a simple conversation.

I would be one of the talkers, despite
the fact that I knew what my talking destroyed.
And so I would mourn every word I said,
even while I argued passionately for silence
and for learning to honor the sacred diversity
of life. Imagine watching the stars
go out on a dark night in the far north, a clear night,
one after the other until the sky went black.

Once, when I was taking out the garbage, just walking
dully across my back yard, a huge bird—
as big as a vulture but glittering and sleek—
rose from the grass and flew into my body,
knocked the breath out of me, then flew up and away
with a powerful pull of its wings. I could hardly

see it in the darkness. Then it was just gone.

To Blow Away like Mist

A man I knew felt sometimes as though a dog
was stuck inside his body, almost as large as he was—
black lab or golden retriever—unable
to move in that cramped dark, yet waiting for something,
listening to the sounds outside him, in the world.

When humans were lost in the rubble of disasters,
dogs like his inner life worked tirelessly—
beyond exhaustion, even to the point of death—
to save the victims, or locate their bodies.
The man knew he wasn't gifted with that kind of vivid selflessness,
that he lacked the keen senses such heroic dogs need.
This realization always opened a great emptiness inside him:

he could let himself seem to blow away then, like mist
in tall grass at dawn before anyone's walked there
or even looked out at it, when the day's breeze rises
and each blade of grass is lifted into clarity,
each stalk standing more taut as it dries,

and the small birds swoop down to disappear there for a moment
then swirl themselves up into the unencumbered sky.

The Ghost Trees

And now a certain kind of scientist says
the weather in various parts of the world
is growing exhausted and just wants to lie down
for a nap, or maybe for a longer dose
of oblivion, so its dreams can be
re-spawned, its creatures large and small
replenished to wildness, the air re-folded
into its invisible origami, even
human language shot-through again
with sap.   In the clear-cut woods—
raw ground and stumps—invisible trees
are learning to move from one place to another,
blurring paths and meadows; the people
who live there call them *fathers who turned*
away without waving goodbye, and learned
to dance slowly; they contrast them with the boulders
and rocks, who truly know how to dance
in slow time, even as the humans and the creatures
in fur and the creatures in feathers leave
their bodies and all the bodies they passed through
to arrive at now through eternities—but still
we pretend they cast shadows across the ground,
and still we pretend they bear fruit.

The Secret Language

After he'd cut the grass, he raked up a dead snake
killed by the mower, and hung what was left of it
on a low branch, then walked around rubbing
his forearms, talking softly to himself.

There were doves in the cut grass, pecking at the insects
the mower had disturbed. And the snake, with its
pink flesh, hung there calling to the flies.

But this is not the truth. If there were children in the house,
they were standing at the windows, or reading in their bedrooms,
on their beds, with their legs jutting straight out, wearing
shoes as though dressed to go somewhere; there was dirt
on the bedspreads, cut grass and twigs, the kind

that stains. Don't worry. Keep reading until
the darkness falls, and your father has to come inside.

By then you all hope he'll be happy again,
that he'll turn on the radio, start taking out the food
from the cupboards and refrigerator, talking in the language
he says he grew up in, that language you will never
understand, even though your brothers and sisters
seem to be fluent, and you speak it in a rush
sometimes, to yourself, like a secret.

The Horses

In that place you never want to talk about, there were
horse skins hanging from nails in the barn
where there once had been horses. You told me your parents

would go in there sometimes and strip each other naked
and slip into those horse skins. You've said their bodies
would seem to grow larger to fill that slack skin

until they were actual horses. And you stood there
in the bare yard waiting for those horses to push open
that barn door with their massive heads and limp off

as though they were overworked and world-weary, out
into the tall grass; their ribs showed gaunt,
their eyes were filmy, and flies made a dark cloud

around their slack bodies, but still they walked out there
while you aired-out the barn, gathered their clothing,
folded it neatly, and set it in a pile

on the bench for later. Then you went inside
to nap and wander though the house. You cooked yourself
a big meal—something you loved—and then you waited

for the moon to rise full through the still afternoon.
And that night you would carry out the saddles and reins,
bit and blinders, or you'd walk out

in your nightgown to ride your mother and father
bareback, until they remembered who they were
by the feel of your small legs around them.

Scarecrow

I spent my youth waking up before my body did,
    walking outside to look around for the animals
that roamed at night. I'd stand until morning,

and then, when I came in for coffee, I'd change
    from something like a window to something like a door
a person could walk through, and close. Sometimes,

even now, when I walk out beyond where I know
    I am who I am, in sleep or that kind
of waking in which there's no language, I stand still

for what seems like years. But I don't flatter
    myself: nothing's scared off. The world has grown up
around me like trees in an unattended field

where once lived a farm, and a family. Soon enough
    those trees will be a forest and I'll just be standing here,
tattered and fading. Birds will land

on my shoulders and arms. They might peck at whatever's
    left of me, seeds or insects. Do I look like
a man now, propped here like a signpost? Sometimes

I wake in my other life and listen to my wife's
    breathing beside me in her sleep, and remember
the dream of those birds on my shoulders, those ravenous

crows I once frightened away, who use me
    as a perch now, a feeder. Soon enough she wakes,
gets up in the pre-dawn darkness, and moves

through the bedroom, making all the smaller birds fly up
    and crash against the ceiling, all the night-creatures
scurry back under the floorboards and be gone

    as she jostles my shoulder, to wake me.

The Blizzard

I was dreaming, I realize now, when I woke for school,
dreaming as I fastened my shirt buttons and zipped up
my pants to go downstairs in the darkness to the kitchen

where my mother was dishing out oatmeal, and the snow
fell outside the big window.
I was dreaming as I pulled on my boots and headed off

through the snow that hadn't been shoveled, into
the morning that wasn't yet light, and I was dreaming
when I arrived at school, earlier than the others,

and walked in a strange sort of silence to my classroom
across the waxed hallway, went in and sat down.
I was still dreaming when the others arrived

but I was not afraid of waking up then. And the teacher
in her dark dress and paper-white skin started braiding
the girls' hair up front, one after the other,

while we all sang a sweet song of cornfields and crows.
I was dreaming, I know that for sure now, when she asked us
to recite what she'd written on the board, but the board

was blank. I spoke anyway, whatever came into
my head and all the other students did too, and so we sang
a new kind of hymn in that early-morning classroom

while the teacher cried softly and the windows
turned gray, the snow falling even harder.

The Truth of Poetry

We were walking through an unfamiliar neighborhood, carrying
a wolf's heart in a basket and looking at the street signs.
There were clouds of dragonflies darkening the sky,
so we felt like we were walking through twilight, though
it was only early afternoon. We'd heard that a wolf's heart

might keep beating for years, and that it might be sewn
into our bodies with no more pain
than a tattoo or a piercing. We imagined we might be made
more nearly immortal if the skin of this heart
were woven into ours, but by the time we found the address
of the veterinarian, the heart

had stopped beating in my hands, and my girlfriend had slipped
into the subway to go home to her family
for dinner. So I carried that dead heart alone
through the city, practicing the many ancient languages

of howling. But silently: I was lost now
and didn't want anyone to find me.

The Light of Ancient Stars

The kid in the newspaper article had calculated
   the number of human beings who'd lived
since the moment the first one emerged from the not-quite-
   human woman who birthed him; the number
was huge, of course, but not nearly as great
   as the number of ants alive in the world
right now, or the billions of bacteria inside
   anyone's body. And his figures suggested
these early people still live inside us,
   grunting their cave-man observations, tasting
the wind tinged with the ichors of long-lost
   creatures who moved like that wind, with light
in their eyes, like ours, creatures that tasted
   so delicious we ate them into oblivion, as merely
by living we extended the great chain of human
   fuckers passed down from that first birth, all
those dreams and hungers leading to *now*
   and on into the future—or veering off slightly
to the side, ignoring what we think of as the *future*
   for something more like the *peripheral*—a river
that branches like a web as it falls, to nurture
   so many different kinds of being,
each with its own way of making a world.
   And then he was quoted as saying how everything
is language and everything speaks, even
   grasses and trees, to make itself real
to itself. Just a kid, still in high school, hardly
   old enough to shave, he claimed his calculations
were just an experiment he'd happened to find himself
   doing one rainy afternoon, instead
of his English homework, which was to finish
   The Scarlet Letter and write a short essay
on secrets and faith, or the vagaries of love.

II.

Constellation

1.
Before we start shooting salt into the sky
to cool the planet and cloud our days,

perhaps we should simply
sit down in the shade
with stories—of moons that break open into flowers,
of foxes that sleep at the foot of our beds
to keep our feet wild. And before we start dreaming

floating cities adrift on a rising
ocean, perhaps we should undress ourselves
of who we've become, slip out of the habits
we've devised to feign our innocence, and swim
out into the deeper water

until whatever's still phosphorescent
within us glows like small constellations
beneath which the huge, warm-blooded swimmers,
with minds and memories, and songs that might teach us
new ways to hear, are moving through the darkness.

2.
Imagine the feel of their huge backs rubbing
against our pale feet, as they move on through the night.

The Shells

As the tide rises, tiny shells
tumble and wait, and tumble. There is nothing
alive inside most of them
but the kind of light
in a room whose curtains have been drawn for years,
a room whose window
faces a street
where people sit late into the evenings at cafés
and the palm fronds flutter. Someone sits quietly
in that room most afternoons, listening
to the chatter, trying to hear a voice
she might recognize. At dusk she gets dressed,
goes down to the café, and drinks a glass of wine.
No one ever talks to her. Of course the ocean never stops
pulling its shells from the deep; some of them
still have creatures alive inside them,
even as they're stranded by the falling tide
to dry up and die, or be eaten by the little birds
who run along the beach, willets or terns,
or picked up by someone who admires their beauty
then throws them back into the ocean.

To Start an Orchard

Whatever silences we'd always maintained
we continued to nurture, like the fruit from a landscape
that was foreign to us, even after all these years,
a fruit we weren't sure whether to peel,
cook, or eat raw, kept on our windowsill
until it had withered and was somehow
beautiful, like a curiosity we'd collected on the beach
that reminded us of journeys, fathomless depths,
and yet was just a piece of fruit, desiccated and black,
curled like the pit of a dream, or a nut.
And so, when you spoke, or tried to, a small plant
emerged from its folds and darkness, delicate
and proud and needing to be watered until
it could be planted outside. I could already
hear the birds singing from its wilderness of branches.
I was already humming to the buzzing of its bees.

The Thieves

My wife and I walked through our quiet neighborhood
collecting mockingbird feathers from the sidewalk
and debating which of our lives had been more
thoroughly wasted, neither of us willing
to admit that those mockingbird feathers might have been
lost for a worrying reason. I could make
a war bonnet with them, I said half facetiously,
or maybe a pair of dress-up wings, for show.
She nodded and changed the topic to the spiderwebs
that quiver in the live oaks, even when there's no breeze,
and catch the most brutal insects, the kind
that inflict us with welts; then she leaned to gather
another mockingbird feather from the sidewalk;
she held it like a bouquet of flowers, or a torch
to light our way home. I held mine in the same way,
to remind her I loved her, and so we marched forward
with purpose and determination, grateful that all
our new wounds seemed to have finally healed,
though the old ones had started barking from the houses
we passed in the dusk-light, like dogs whose masters
were coming home late again, and thought we must be thieves.

The Edge of the World

Let's imagine a woman could walk to the edge
of the world as we know it, sit down there to rest
and look out over what we think of as nothing
while she waits for her husband to arrive with the supplies.
Or perhaps she doesn't wait and just keeps walking,
wondering whether she might simply disappear.
She's the kind of woman who gives a dollar to the homeless guy
as though it's just a loan; she's the kind of person
who gathers up stray cats and takes them to the pound
so the wild birds will be safe in her garden.
Now she walks into nothing at the edge of the world,
and it's not what you'd expect from the stories of conquistadores
hacking out the jungle for its gold. No, she finds herself
sitting in a café drinking cappuccino
and talking to someone who looks like he could be
a door into a room full of light, in a house
so perfect she'd dissolve there, or explode like tiny bubbles
in a glass of champagne, as her husband stands confused
back at the edge there, calling her name
until he gives up, turns around and goes home
to find someone like her, someone he doesn't know
though everything about her is familiar, as though
he'll never wake again. And so he lives by dreaming.

The Skin

The language you gave up
    when you moved to this country
waits underground
    patiently for spring,

like a snake that will whip
    across the scrubby yard
to wake you some morning
    to what you're really thinking.

You'll find its sloughed skin
    and carry it inside.
Softer than an infant's breath,
    it smells like happiness

and whispers in a language
    which fits another dream,
of someone from some other life
    who's thinking of you now.

The Afternoon Nap

You fall asleep in the library and wake up on a train
in a landscape you remember from *Doctor Zhivago*,
a film you saw more than once, many years ago,
but have mostly forgotten. You've been studying the nuances
of late-Romantic thought, trying not to dwell
on your fiancée's distraction; lately she laughs
with far less abandon than she used to, before
your proposal. You remember the horses
in that very long movie. Weren't there wolves too?
They mostly stayed hidden in the woods, though now
you can see them through the trees. You point, though there's no one
to follow your finger. You should have worn a warmer coat,
you think, rocking gently as the train pushes on
through miles of untracked snow, toward a place you've never been
but remember now, vaguely, from the movie, and with
a growing sense that what you've yearned for at the bottom
of your life, in the muck you hardly ever dive
down to—it's hard to hold your breath that long—
is something like the landscape you are entering now,
where it snows all the time and the lakes are frozen solid
and where your fiancée waits beautifully, like
that dark-haired woman in the movie I've already
mentioned you can't remember very well,
though you sat in the darkness and watched her as a boy,
more than once, and felt things there aren't any words for,
even now. Soon the train will stop
at some station you can only imagine; you'll get up
and walk off into that snowy place, into
a language you speak with sudden fluency. She'll be
standing there waiting for you, not as beautiful
as you remember, but crying with joy
and holding up the baby you'd almost completely
forgotten was yours. And he'll be crying too.

Tango

There's wind inside everything, my acupuncturist said
    as she stuck me with a needle—even in the heart,
let's say, of that woman standing beside you
    in the elevator, who steps out at your floor and saunters
briskly down the hall just in front of you, as if
    she were in charge, then turns and asks
if you know where you're going, and if so will you
    point to the right door. But you're lost too, so you tell her
she looks like an old friend's sister, and ask
    how he's doing these days. She frowns and claims
her brother sailed over the horizon and drowned
    in his own solitude, until he saw the whales
and mermaids—she winks then—and couldn't come home
    after that, so he sings to her now through the phone
in a foreign language. It's another form of tango
    she says as she holds out her hand, in that fluorescent
corridor, looks you in the eyes and starts to move
    like a dancer from a country where passion is all
that matters, and you scowl back as though you thought that too.

The Lesson

Our teacher was showing us where we all lived,
on a map at the front of the room. She was pointing
with a yardstick and telling us how her parents came
on a boat across the ocean, how they didn't speak English
and ate different kinds of vegetables and fruits
than we ate here, and she named them: *eggplant,
pepper, radish*—but I'd eaten all those foods
and my parents grew up in Brooklyn, so what was she
trying to tell us? She pointed to the wall
and talked on and on as the snow fell, clicking
against the windows, until someone—a kid
whose face I can't remember, who wore
a checkered shirt, and glasses—walked over
to that window and opened it wide: a gust
of freezing wind and slush burst in
to cover his face and make him look
like a snowman for a moment when he turned to us, laughing.
The teacher just talked on, naming different soups,
different kinds of fruit juice while the whole class lined up
at the windows to look out at the boy—whose name
I already told you I don't remember—
as he climbed down the fire escape, without
a jacket, and walked off across the playground
toward a clutch of shadows that might have been dogs
and paced back and forth at the far edge, near the trees.

The Retreat

In the life that runs parallel to this one, I'd bought
a small acreage of woods, with trails and a swimming hole,
a place to retreat to, to "find myself" in
and to look up at the stars. But when we took a walk there
at the start of our sojourn, we found spiderwebs draped
between the branches of each tree; many were filled
with small birds whose flapping only tightened the strands
and suffocated them. They must have been migrating,
I thought, since I'd never seen such lovely birds
around here. Whoever I was walking with took out
a clipboard and started making a list
of the caught birds, recording their thrashings and death-songs
with her phone. When I reached up to free a bird, she scowled
and told me not to touch it. And when I asked why not,
she simply turned away. As she walked she let her clothes fall—
she dropped each item like a flower—until
she was naked. "Come in," she said then, "and I'll teach you
about spiderwebs and songbirds, and soon you'll begin
to understand this country where you've bought a little land,
city boy. Touch me. . ." But I couldn't, although
she was beautiful as any wild thing. Instead I turned back,
retracing my steps, noticing her clothes
on the path were just bread crumbs, not flowers. And when I reached up
to untangle a struggling bird from the web
that had clenched it in a death-grip, it fell away to dust
as the gummy strands tightened around my outstretched hands
and held me firmly planted there, reaching up into that tree.

First Love

There was grass growing through the weave in her sweater,
pushing out at her wrists, up over her collar.
She was sitting on a rock, and talking to me
about feathers, how they're dreamed in the egg,
how they start out as hollow straws, like hay,
how they turn to flowers, and finally feather
into feathers; she was talking so softly

I had to lean close, and I saw that the grass
that pushed through her clothing was richly green,
like a pelt—not like the tall grass of the meadow
that surrounded us. I had wandered off
the familiar trail through the woods where we'd played
hide-and-seek, and where I'd gathered branches
for a fire. I'd just wanted to explore

by myself for once. There was mica in the stone
she sat on but there were no birds in the trees.
My teeth felt like pebbles in my mouth, and my speech
was garbled when I tried to tell her I was lost,
so she didn't understand. Let me tell you the truth:

when she took off her sweater and jeans and stood there
before me, I could see her body,
as pale as ivory or the moon, beneath
the lush grass that covered her, that had been ripped
and torn a little when she stripped herself naked.
There were wildflowers too. I was just a boy,
though I knew about yearning. And then she lay down
without a single word. Do you understand me now?
She turned away and lay herself down then as grass.

Routine Weather

When I reach home, I take off my sweats, release
my undirected weather, empty the trash cans
and make the many beds that are tumbled and tossed
in the bedrooms inside me; then I drain the black oil
and muzzle the guard dogs, who take themselves out
for a walk while I cook up my socks and old shoes,
humming an anthem I played for my friends
in the dorm room—about freedom and dusty back roads
to nowhere but some hobo's secondhand life
while I made up a career. It was there, I realize,
that I lost the leather jacket that seemed to make me interesting,
those slick boots whose heels won me arguments, that hat
that made my long hair flow like potency itself
while I moaned the blues like a field hand and headed
reluctantly off to my day job delivering
flowers to secretaries screwed by their bosses
and housewives screwed by the suburbs. So I sit here
naked as a chicken leg steaming on a dinner plate,
a man sliding free of his sleeping bag naked
as an earthworm, who stands now and walks through the trees
looking for a path to the picnic and wondering
whether that whispering in the distance is a waterfall
or just another ravenous machine.

The Lion

Who is this version of someone else's idea
of a life, with rain pouring in through the window
and rain pouring down from the ceiling, while the TV
blares cop shows, and birds shaped like private facts-of-life
fly around, shitting on the open books
and on this man's head when he's sleeping? Always
the scent of hot plastic, always the bleeding
fingernails, the mushrooms in the closets and the slow hair
that curls up beneath the bare mattress covered
with dandruff that glitters in morning light.
And when I was a lion, he tells himself now,
I could make my friends dare their heads into my mouth.
That felt like happiness. And when I was a seal
I didn't mind swimming in circles—so he walks around
the living room until he's exhausted and lies down
to pretend he's a flower for the rest of the day,
ignoring the bees of his own imagination,
the honey they make from his body, the pollen
they gather from his eyelashes, the nectar they taste
on his breath and in his eyes as they fly off into
the window-glass and fall to the carpet, stunned
but still buzzing. Eventually he'll seem to wake
like a photograph might, unable to move,
and he'll lie there remembering all the good times he's had
in his life, which are somewhere off in the distance,
preening, preparing to roar.

The Windows

Everything's a window the professor told my class,
and I thought about breaking that glass, or shutting
the curtains—or better yet opening those windows
and climbing out into the snowy world beyond.
He said fashioning windows *is the only way*
we can make sense of what we see, so even
as I walked off through that snow I must have made windows.
Pretty soon I found a road, plowed clean and gleaming black,
between those walls of snow, and I walked, not the least bit
chilly, imagining I would find something
eventually. And soon a big dog came bounding up.
I smelled wood smoke. Imagine discovering a village
full of people who seem to know you, at the end
of a long road, out in a wilderness of snow!
I stepped inside a house whose first floor was a dark bar,
warm and crowded with bearded men
who raised their glasses as I entered, beckoned me
to sit by the fire, and asked if I was having
the usual. I'd been lonely forever
I realized as the barmaid brought my soup and beer
with a wink that felt genuine. I was starving, so I ate
without stopping, through the night, and then I slept, in a room
with curtained windows behind which many birds
were singing, as though teaching me another way to wake.

The Mica-Daughter

Sure, we could ask our *true selves* to slice open
the clouds hanging in our closets, and let
the memories of summer afternoon thunderstorms
sweeten our shoes; we could throw open our windows
to let the waves rush in; sure, we could awaken
the surfboards sleeping in their narrow cots
and ride from wind to breeze to breath—

or we could practice the instruments we've never
mastered: tweezers and dental floss, toothbrush
and broken-toothed comb; we could learn how to stroke
harmonics by grooming our middle-aged physiognomies

if it weren't for afternoons like this one, when a man
called father gets caught in the window, and fades
into something like the skin of our eyes as we watch
the trees fill with dusk and the cars move their passengers
up and down the streets, when we can't help seeing
a crow who looks like our mother out there
nodding at the window. But then she's just a stump
by the time we arrive. It's like the smell of glass
in winter, a mirror filled with frozen rain,

as the brother, our brother, holds something like a howl
inside his shadow. Soon enough he's only
the smell of a tooth buried under a pillow
by a wolf-child with an old soul, the son who sings
pop songs backward and is chosen as a holy man
by his crossing guard, his teachers, and his friends, yet his friends
are afraid of the charms he weaves with the wind
to make himself something like grass-kneeling-down,
long hair of the bodies imprisoned underground,

as you are imprisoned in the girl of this family,
Sweet Sally of the Almost-There, who glistens like mica
and breaks things to mend them, to break them and mend them
again by stitching or gluing, staples
or nails. When you clap she'll vanish. But listen:
truly she has never been; truly, she is mica
at the center of our days, that sharpens our bones
and lights those faces in the photograph albums
we consult to remember our lives, until eventually

we've misplaced what glinted. By then we're just lost light.

Nature Poem

> *I'm wondering how to fill it, that sack you left me*
> *of sky, redundant as an egg...*
> —Bill Berkson

Something like a swarm of bees inside the air,
        something like a mattress full of quills, or a tee shirt
                glistening with fish scales sloughed from the body
      of a man who blistered his fingers on the clouds
he leaped to grab onto, as though he could become them,
        so he could be rainfall. This is the grief
                of wool hats in the tropics, or a bone in the river
        that's been smoothed into a pebble. You pick it up and wonder
what the wind might intend as it worries the trees—

        but wind intends nothing, of course, like that pebble
                falling through the ocean inside you, behind your
      rib bones and moon-bone and closets full of blaring
ambulance-street-cars and broken fire trucks
        hoping to rescue the snakes from your shoes
                before they start sliding up your legs like vines
      to poke into your holes. So I lean to read your palm,
close enough to smell that perfume you've sprayed
        on your clothes and hair as though that might make you
                less mortal. And it does, at least while the fevers
      are rising inside us and our fingers are stroking
that fur; at least while our barefoot dances
        continue long after the music's gone limp
                and the rain has reminded us again of the silence

        always inside, like the lake we dive into,
so crowded the with arm-length ravenous fish
        we think of as *sheriffs of the ocean*, though
                they're caught here in fresh water, sluggish with thirst
      and yearning for salt. But we let them devour us
anyway, the way a man might turn into
        the cat he petted, and purr his way into
                oblivion while his wife sat at home
      watching old sitcoms and picking at her fingernails
until they were bleeding, then doing push-ups
        until she broke down and cried out   dirt
                will be dirt.   Remember: those fish weren't fooled
      by the flies you tied with your father, leaning

    in the near-dark basement workroom, while
        your mother took her clothes off in the kitchen upstairs,
            lay down on the floor and dreamed she might melt
    into a skeleton to demonstrate just how

a fish might shiver. Soon there was glittering
    glass in the path you walked, barefoot,
        thinking you might still escape the relentless
    dogs in your body—large dogs that howled
like wolves and were always ravenous, until
    your bare feet left blood prints all over the floor
        beside your mother, while your father took a shower
    and sang in the voice of Ella Fitzgerald
or Bessie Smith, if they could have sung
    like a man who sang like a woman, off key,
        and the walls started sweating as the rain seeped through
    the wallpaper your mother had hung, pictures
of fruits that have never existed, and carrots,
    interspersed with small mammals—bunnies and squirrels—
        cute creatures, while off in the distance the farmhouse
    waited so patiently it almost made you cry
as the horses and pigs there exploded, one by one.

The Pure Necessity

Written in response to the art of Anselm Kiefer

    . . .the way the river rises
while we're sleeping, and floods our bedroom—and carries
    our house out into the current, into
the deeps, where the ancient creatures live;

        the way we fall asleep together every night
to a moaning train or a cop show; the way we wake up
    many years later
        to the bird no one has named
knocking its head at our window:

        your memories
live beyond your body, and prove to the trees
    there's really no such thing as *dreaming*—

        just as there might be nothing called wind
        if you're moving inside it.

So take this bone, this human fibula, to gnaw
    instead of growing old like an idea does; break
this raw bone, then bury it under your belt
or boil it for years, until someone calls it soup
    and you're free of pretending yourself into another,
    and you're free to climb those secret stairs, up into the clouds,
        to explode there like rain,
        to make the river rise.

You think yourself raw and find only one answer:
    refuse to consider angels wearing coats
        of wax or lard, the Great Mother your image
    of what is so real it lacks meaning.

        The first trees
    were prayers he explained to us then, whose leaves
        were pressed into oil and charcoal.

They contained a secret knowledge only angels ever spoke:

    . . .flat men on the balcony facing away
into the sun, to accelerate the transformation
    that makes nothing solid, but real.

                                        Dear Angels,
I know you as wonder, objects the mind
            intuits from its past lives, the touch of a burning
                        finger, fairy-tale sunflowers—a massive wall
            built of old train ties—*sleepers*—their bodies
still potent with living oils, a green-dust smell, the lives

            those trees lived for centuries, the oxygen they made.

Each time we see them, a spark of ancient flickers,
            and each time we see them   the breezes come alive
                        between us, as when we really see

                                    we come alive again

      in the pure necessity of mind we call *soul*
                  so we can forget it, embarrassed at the word—

and this is what we humans do—attend to our own minds

                  as a means of forgetting, a letting go
            of the big world of rocks and angels and trees,
shapes that sing like magic wands
            or sparklers children swirl like halos
                        around their heads, as the evening settles down

like a huge flock of black birds
we'd thought were extinct—

                  or maybe that's just bees buzzing through the flowers,
            reminding us always

                  of honey.

                                    *

In a room of rubble and brittle light,
            I suddenly know things I'll never understand:
each moment is an animal, leaping sunlight
                  to give us these bodies. You touched me. I opened

a window and was suddenly
        lost outside

so I sang as a way of hiding in the words
        until my first parents were forgotten, my father
        who danced like a breaking wave, my mother
            who hung her dresses in a closet and sealed
        the closet, painted it as though it were a wall

and walked away. But I was still inside—

        I understand the rubble we must crawl through
            to make the world again, as the moon grows full
        above us, and hangs like a blister while we sleep—

        a dirty fingernail reflecting dusty light—

        as dresses rise up like wings into the darkness
inside us, full of satellites mapping out our landscapes

as though we weren't *real* at all, and plotting out our minds.

        —for Richard Blanco & John William Bailly

III.

The House

She folds a piece of typing paper
into a house. Let's live here, she says,
as she makes herself tiny. I follow, and we enter

lives that feel suddenly new, surrounded
by walls and ceiling so drenched in light
we squint as we look at each other.

Our new house lacks windows, so we watch the walls
for shadows. Soon we'll have to scissor some doors
so we can move around outside again

but for now we're content with each other and the white
walls and our shadows against the white walls,
which move as though we were dancing.

Soup

I'm trying to remember how to make your favorite soup
when I have only candles and soap and it's raining
hard enough to feel we are living underwater
or at least behind a waterfall. Could I use my own skin?
Tears are warm and salty, but I don't want to cry
just to make your soup; that seems faintly histrionic
or at least sentimental. The best soup's made with bones,
of course, and I haven't any fresh ones, at least not outside
my body. So I think of many things
I don't feel anymore, and of you trudging
home now in this historic rain, maybe even humming
one of our favorite songs under your breath,
thinking of my soup as you take a wrong turn
in the deluge, almost tasting that soup as you wade
the sidewalk-rapids on a street in some neighborhood
that looks a lot like ours, though it isn't. I am boiling
clear water now, just to find you.

The Adjustment

When we moved my study down from the attic
to the empty bedroom our children used to share,
we built new bookshelves from branches we collected
in the backyard. It was a kind of sculpture,
interesting to look at, but difficult to balance
the books in, and the branches swarmed with bugs.
Before long, insects were eating my library,
and when I sat down in the evening after work
with a favorite book of poetry, chiggers bit my arms,
leaving welts I scratched until they bled, so when
I hugged my wife, I left blood on her clothes.
There was blood all over our sheets in the morning.
Eventually I simply stopped reading, a logical
solution to the problem. I'm happy now
to spend my days up in the attic—where the old
bookshelves stand empty—strumming the guitar
I bought way back in college and played
for my dormitory comrades, high on pot and friendship.
I fumble through those old songs without my youthful grace
and I can't hit the high notes, but it feels like happiness
and no one else is listening, so I let myself wail on.

The Pond

If I claimed I grew up in a house made real
by the songs my father sang as he moved
from room to room, songs he made up
to make the furniture solid and keep
the windows holding the wind, and if I
told you I sat in my room and cried
when he fell finally silent, I'd have to
sing in my own voice to fill up the silence
he left us, if I wanted to keep things
whole—and I know so few songs that are *mine*
and I know the whole house is listening.
So I start singing, just singing, and the songs
begin to move like breeze through the house.
If I told you my brother is dancing as he listens,
in the bedroom we share, my sister chattering
to keep my voice distant, my mother would be lying
in bed, dreaming of holding my father,
who slept like a hole in the ground beside her,
a cave that filled slowly with pure water when it rained—
cool, refreshing curtains of wetness
falling as we slept, to fill up the emptiness
gaping beside her and make a small pond
we could swim in, together again,
whenever that rain stopped falling.

The Dance

And speaking of silence, one night I slid
        a canoe off the rack and paddled out to see
what swans looked like in the darkness, folded
        into themselves, asleep.

Soon I was lost in the marshes, caught
        in the pull of tide. I couldn't see anything
but tall grass and stars, and it took all night
        to locate my shore. When I got home at dawn

I slipped into bed, pretending to wake up
        an hour later, to find my parents
in the kitchen discussing the thrashing they'd heard
        at the edge of their sleep: was it a hawk

or an owl? Then I was slipping out
        most nights to search for swans, returning
at dawn to my parents in the kitchen as I sat down
        to breakfast and started recounting my dreams,

made up on the spot, as the darkness outside
        lightened and another ordinary morning
brightened our kitchen. Sometimes my mother
        turned on the radio while she cooked

and we listened to the music she loved, soft
        waltzes and folk songs she danced to sometimes—
just a few steps—when she thought I wasn't watching,
        since my plate was piled high with food, but once

I noticed my dad catch her eye, and they smiled
        with a lightness that turned them to children
I'd never met. And then that moment passed
        as they sat down, grunting, to eat.

The Stars

Sometimes, my girlfriend told me, her mother
slept through the day, waking only
toward evening, to get all spiffy, drive
around the block, come back in and say
her work had been exhausting: she shouldn't be disturbed.

Other days, her mother really went to the office
but didn't come home; in fact sometimes
she was gone for a week. And when she finally
returned, wearing fancier clothes
than the ones she'd left in, she acted as though
she'd kissed my girlfriend goodbye just that morning
as she asked about the hamster and turtle, pets
that had died years earlier.

This girl loved to play make-believe and sing
gibberish songs. She also knew
the names of the snakes and mushrooms in our region
and she claimed to be an expert on weather patterns too.

When her dad took us out in his boat one afternoon,
he ventured out farther than he'd been before,
and when it came time to return to our harbor,
we realized we were lost.

We kept studying the shoreline for buildings we recognized
and he kept assuring us everything was fine
despite the evening settling around us
and the fact that we were running out of gas.

When the engine finally died and we started
drifting toward shore in the dark, my girlfriend—
whose teeth were chattering by now—started naming
the stars, which seemed to grow brighter as she spoke
and the darkness deepened behind them.

The Apple Trees

Your mother loved waking late, after everyone else
in the family was gone so the house could relax
around her, and a kind of smoke
could fill her rooms with silence and the smell
of tanned leather saddles on the horses she rode
around and around as a child while her father
in his bow-tie watched from the car, smoking
a pipe, with the window rolled down, and planned
his gardens of turtles and birdbaths and cool
terraces laughing with drinks at dusk
and new-mown grass, while she cantered, pondering
boys in general and seashells so deep
no one will ever find them or marvel
at their beauty, put them on display and imagine
what lived so many miles underwater
the dark there is permanent, like the sap inside a memory
of apple trees bursting into flames we could gather
and give as a gesture of love, for their fragrance,
or listen to the bees there and watch their fruit ripen,
or climb them in an ancient story, up into the sky.

The Deer

It had snowed all night. By early afternoon
a blizzard was howling, with winds that seemed
to shiver the walls of our high school, where the students
in the co-ed gym class were bounding up and down
the basketball court with kick-balls we threw
at each other and up toward the ceiling, laughing.
It might have been the wildness of the blizzard, but even
the coaches seemed to have relaxed
as the windows darkened with winter's early dusk.
And, yes, I was there, as though in some other life,
kicking and running, when someone noticed
a *deer* by the gym-door, shaggy with snow,
and another, with antlers, behind him. They slowly

approached us with delicate steps across
the polished wood floor, while we watched, silent,
still flushed from our game. Then the smaller deer
danced through the crowd of our sweaty bodies
as though slipping deftly through an overgrown wood,
or like a fish might slide through a crowd of swimmers.
Its larger companion stood watching.

They walked across the gym, dripping clumps of snow,
and out the back door. We followed, to see
a herd of deer, at least twenty, ambling
down the otherwise empty fluorescent
hallway, filling the hall with their snowy
bodies, stopping to lick the walls,
pulling off the posters and drawings with their teeth
and leaning to eat them. When they saw us,

they paused for a moment, drew into a huddle,
and leapt, one by one, out the high window
they must have leapt through to come in. Then
they were simply gone.

            That night, after walking
home alone along the unplowed streets,
after helping my father dig the car from a drift,
as I lay in my warm bed knowing there would be
no school the next day, I cried. I don't know
exactly why—perhaps at the way
that smaller deer had wended its way through the crowd
of our bodies, or at the way those deer had leapt
so gracefully through that small, high window,
one after the other, how they had waited
so patiently to leap, the beauty of their leaping.

I must have sobbed loudly, since my mother came in
with a flashlight—the power was out—and sat
on my bed and sang a lullaby as she
stroked my hair back. Now listen: I knew
I was too big to cry; in fact I was almost
a man, and wouldn't they all have laughed,
my school friends, if they'd seen me lying there
crying like a little kid, some kind of blubbering
baby?

            The snow kept falling through the night,
like a whispered conversation in an unwritten tongue
we know in our bodies but will never understand,
impossible and perfect as silence.

The Lucky One

Summer evenings, when thousands of fireflies
rose from the cool grass, we'd catch them in jars
that made them suddenly ordinary.

Sometimes, when we killed one by mistake,
our mother would save it for later, after
we'd gone to bed. She'd study it then

at the kitchen table, glasses perched
at the end of her nose, squinting as she leaned close,
then looking up to blink and sip

her nightcap, while our father listened
to Monk or Bud Powell, loud when he was
a little drunk, which made us children

hold our pillows tight to our heads
and wake up grumpy next morning.

*

In those days ragged men haunted the trains
that ran between the city and the suburbs.

Sometimes one would sit down beside me
to tell me his stories, and though I'd pretend
to be reading intently, I'd listen, innocent
boy that I was then, privileged kid
who'd never be drafted, or forced to sign up
for anything, really, I didn't want to do.

Later, as I lay in bed, I'd listen
to the animals I imagined were moving through the dark,
timid creatures who knew how to vanish
from the day like a man might vanish from his own life.

Sometimes, unable to sleep, I wandered
outside and stood there as though those night creatures
might approach me, open the doors of their houses
and invite me inside until morning.

*

Warm afternoons, our father threw a tennis ball
out into the harbor for our black Lab, Charlie,
until Charlie's mouth was bleeding, and our father
was laughing in exhaustion—still Charlie begged for more.
He barked as swans flew over that harbor,
touching the tips of their wings sometimes
to the dirty water. That was the year

a girl I'd had a crush on was infected when she dipped
her feet in that water and died before
she made it to the hospital.
                                        And if I woke up
sometimes in the middle of the night to Charlie's
moaning in his sleep, and woke my brother
in the bunk above me, and we slipped into our sister's
room to make sure she was fine, and if
we moved down the hall to our parents' bedroom,
stood still there and listened to their breathing,

what more could we do to protect them? Sometimes
my brother slid into bed beside me
and we listened to each other's breathing as we slept.
Sometimes in the morning, still groggy, we tried
to tell each other what we'd dreamt, whatever
snippets we remembered, if we remembered anything,
but more often we got dressed in silence.

The Tree

stands there crying like a man who thinks
nothing memorable will ever happen
to him again, because it's filled
with gleaming crows
disturbed by a change
in the taste of the air. And I can't quite see
from this distance what kind of tree it is
though I notice the house behind it looks
like a farmhouse from some other century.
If I squint, I can see horses in the fields
beyond the house. That tree is really
crying now, and as I lean
to listen, I realize with growing alarm
it's not the *tree* crying but someone inside
that farmhouse, someone whose voice I think
I must recognize. So I call back, like a crow.
And then another crow joins in, and another,
until all I can hear is our own incessant cawing.
The house might as well be silent.

The Falls

He was standing on a branch in the middle of the river
calling my name. But that river, swift
as it is there, shallow and narrow, is easy

to wade across. So I turned away
without thinking: we'd come all that way
for solitude and stars, and so he and I might talk

after so many years. But then I glanced up
to see he was wading away from me, down
to the edge of those falls, moving like he needed

to get somewhere quickly, though perhaps that was just
the swifter current, and the deeper water
in that stretch of the river, and he'd simply decided

to stop fighting its power, and let himself just go.

The Shirt

I thought I heard a man muttering
    in the next cubicle: someone he loved
had gotten hopelessly lost, and everyone seemed
    to just want to move on. But where would they go,
he wondered. The shirt fit well,

    so I stepped out to find my wife and get
her approval. Then we could go home and putter
    in the yard, and none too soon: stores
like that make me anxious, alarmed at the sheer
    amount of *stuff* in the world, and this man—

whoever he was—had reminded me of someone
    I'd been once, of someone I'd lost.
When I couldn't find her, I asked another woman
    what she thought of the shirt, I smiled and held
my arms out like an amateur model, but she

    just gazed blankly into the air
like I wasn't even there, and I was left
    smiling at emptiness, wearing that beautiful
shirt, and holding my arms out as though
    waiting for someone to hug me. Or to dance.

The 20th Century

The engineers who knew how to improve our lives
flooded this valley of hill farms and small towns
and called it a lake. They stocked it with fish,

and soon our traditions were born, these speedboats
and vacation cottages, while deep down in the darkness:
the farms and stores and houses, some of which
still held cans of food in their cupboards,
clothes in their closets, albums heavy
with photographs, and trucks in their yards.

There were people down there too, the people who'd refused
to leave, who'd locked their doors, laid down
on their cots and waited for the river to rise.

—Today, if you paddle out into the middle
and drop a pebble, it might settle, far below,
on the back porch of a small house built by the man
whose bones lie inside, still wearing the clothes
he lay down in. His wife lies beside him.

Your pebble might take an hour to drift
to the bottom, that's how deep the lake is,
by which time you'll be doing something else, on shore,
living in your mind that is like that deep water
with the sinking pebble and the dead man lying there.

Sometimes in winter, when the lake freezes,
the children skate out with their parents.
As they hold hands and chatter, every gleeful exclamation
is visible for a moment, rising up into the air.

The Journey Home

When I finally summoned the urge to go home
after all these years, I couldn't remember
exactly how to get there, though I did know how to find
the train. I filled a bag with small gifts
for all my old friends, though I couldn't remember
exactly who they were—what I mean is I couldn't
remember who'd died: chocolate and nice-smelling
soap, things everyone loves. I was dreaming
already of how they would all blush and clap
to see who I was now. There were no empty seats,
so I stood. Presently someone got up
and hurried from the car, then another jumped up,
then two more, and so on until the train
was empty, though of course all those slobs
had left their garbage behind—cups
and newspapers, wrappers of who knows what.
So I leaned down the aisle picking up their junk,
I kneeled down and swept it from under their seats,
marveling at all the good stuff they'd chucked.
Then I sat down to read the old newspapers I'd piled
beside me on the seat, my ticket safely tucked
into my front pocket, as the lights flickered
and the doors finally slid shut, sighing.
The train gave a shiver then as though it felt the cold.
It groaned like it knew something I didn't. You know
the kind of groan I mean? *No train can make that sound,*
you're probably thinking. But you are very wrong.
And soon we were moving through the darkness.

*

Starting from Sleep

    She tells me our bodies are nets dropped into
the ocean. And when they are pulled up, the minnows
are spilled out to flip-flop and strangle.

    And then we are tossed back over, to dream:

> *I talk,* she says, *to my great-great-grandchildren*
>   *by treating all things with whatever compassion*
> *I've drawn from the grace I've been shown. And those children*
>   *thank me, and dream of being born.*

The wild parts of everything are disappearing everywhere.

        Wood grain faint fingerprint
            pores eyes blue breathing
      wind dust mind afternoon
              tide lips   and sudden flowers.

Thanks to Jesse Millner for reading innumerable drafts and revisions and to Tom Virgin for making art out of my jottings.

Thanks also to the editors and publishers of my earlier books, particularly Rick Campbell and Lynne Knight (Anhinga Press), Alan Davis (New Rivers Press), Richard Mathews (University of Tampa Press), Scott King (Red Dragonfly Press), Gary Metras (Adastra Press), the late Robert Bixby (March Street Press), Bob and Susan Arnold (Longhouse), and Jay Snodgrass (Hysterical Press).

Thanks to Lola Haskins, Richard Jones, Anne Marie Macari and Al Maginnes for their generous endorsements.

Heartfelt thanks to Kevin Morgan Watson, who responded to my out-of-the-blue email query with a stunning generosity that is as beautiful as it is rare. It is an honor to work with a publisher of his caliber. My gratitude extends in equal measure to Christopher Forrest, certainly the most thorough, sympathetic, nuanced and supportive editor I have had the pleasure of working with. His editorial insights improved this book immeasurably.

Thanks to the Florida Division of Cultural Affairs for Fellowships in Poetry.

As always, my greatest gratitude goes to my wife and truest love, Colleen.

Michael Hettich was born in Brooklyn, NY, and grew up in New York City and its suburbs. He has lived in upstate New York, Colorado, Northern Florida, Vermont, Miami, and Black Mountain, North Carolina, where he now lives with his family. He has published over a dozen books and chapbooks of poetry, and his work has appeared widely in journals and anthologies. His awards include several Florida Individual Artists Fellowships, a Florida Book Award, The Tampa Review Prize in Poetry, and the David Martinson–Meadow Hawk Prize. He often collaborates with visual artists, musicians, and fellow writers. He is married to Colleen and has two children, Matthew and Caitlin.

Cover artist Jim Muehlemann is a recipient of the Prix de Rome from the American Academy in Rome. He has also received a grant from the Adolph and Ester Gottlieb Foundation. Prior to the professorship that he now holds at Randolph College, Jim lived in New York City for twenty years, where he had numerous one-person exhibitions. He continues to show his work throughout the country. Jim lives with his wife Kathy in Lynchburg, Virginia.

www.ingramcontent.com/pod-product-compliance
Lightning Source LLC
LaVergne TN
LVHW041345080426
835512LV00006B/627